CHAPTER ONE

FINANCIAL FREEDOM

What does it truly mean to be financially free? To some, it's living comfortably with the ability to explore the world on a whim, while for others, it's about retiring early with a hefty bank balance. Whatever your version of financial freedom is, it all begins with setting achievable and practical goals.

In your quest for financial independence, you've ventured into the world of rental property investments, and that's a commendable step towards securing a brighter financial future. However, success in this domain isn't a mere stroke of luck; it requires a well-thought-out plan and a mindset to achieve your aspirations.

Before diving into the world of rental property investments, you must build a sturdy foundation of knowledge. Specialized understanding of real estate topics will empower you to make informed decisions and avoid costly mistakes.

Defining Your Purpose: What Do You Seek from Rental Property Investment?

At the core of your pursuit of financial freedom lies a single, overarching goal. Take a moment to ponder what you genuinely desire from rental property investments. Is it the liberty to travel without financial constraints? Maybe you yearn to fortify your retirement account or break free from the chains of a traditional job. Identifying your purpose is vital, as it will fuel your determination throughout this journey.

Steering Clear of Common Rental Property Pitfalls

Without the right knowledge and preparation, mistakes are bound to occur. Some of the most prevalent pitfalls include hiring an inept property manager, hesitating to evict non-paying tenants, investing in properties that drain your resources with maintenance costs, and rushing into deals solely based on tempting prices. A sturdy foundation of knowledge is vital to avoid these pitfalls.

Mastering the Path to Financial Freedom

Success in rental property investment (or any endeavor) lies in adopting six crucial strategies: fostering growth, cultivating a reliable network, prioritizing efficiency, challenging assumptions, establishing clear plans, and nurturing the right mindset. By focusing on growth, you'll make strategic decisions to propel your business forward. A robust network of contacts is indispensable, as success in this domain relies on a collaborative effort.

Efficiency plays a significant role in outsourcing tasks beyond your expertise, while questioning assumptions ensures you remain adaptable and open to innovation. Your well-structured plans will lay the groundwork for financial freedom, guiding your actions towards your ultimate goals. Yet, the most pivotal aspect remains your mindset.

The Power of Mindset: Forging Your Path to Financial Freedom

Transforming your mindset is pivotal. From an early age, we are conditioned to believe that only conventional 9-to-5 jobs lead to success. However, the advent of the e-commerce revolution has opened up new avenues, allowing for remote work and freelancing.

As we explore the potential of passive income streams like rental properties, cultivating the right mindset becomes paramount.

Embrace the idea that rental property investing is more than just a goal—it should be a "burning desire," a singular focus for your studies and efforts. Craft a plan that aligns with your goals and takes you closer to financial freedom each day.

In rental property investments, five key elements work in your favor: cash flow, appreciation, tax benefits, rental income, and inflation. This diversified approach sets you on a journey of long-term success, where patience and the right mindset are indispensable.

As you tread the path towards financial freedom, remember that patience is paramount. Accomplish small daily goals, even during stagnant market periods. Trust that the right opportunity will reveal itself when the time is right.

Elevating Your Mindset for Enduring Triumph

Your voyage towards financial freedom commences with the right mindset. Embrace the e-commerce revolution, and with each stride, you'll find yourself inching closer to your dreams. No more living paycheck to paycheck. With the proper mindset and unwavering determination, rental property investments could lead you to an early retirement, adventurous escapades, or the luxury car you've always yearned for.

Together, let's embark on this transformative journey, learning from one another and adapting as we grow. Each chapter will furnish you with the knowledge and confidence to set sail towards the life you've always envisioned.

Remember, success is not merely about setting goals; it's about nurturing a mindset that propels you towards financial freedom. Let's make this journey extraordinary.

CHAPTER TWO

THE POWER OF RENTAL PROPERTY INVESTMENTS

Unlocking the potential for success in rental property investment begins with a clear understanding of your purpose and the qualities that define a prosperous investor. Let's embark on a journey of self-discovery and explore the mindset, skills, and attributes that will lead you to enduring success in this dynamic field.

Qualities to Embrace for Rental Property Investment

Time Mastery: Effectively managing your time will enable you to prioritize tasks, stay focused, and seize opportunities promptly.

Prospect Pros: Nurturing the ability to spot potential investment opportunities and leads is essential for real estate success.

The Follow-Up Ace: Timely follow-up with leads and

clients is crucial to closing successful deals and building lasting relationships.

The Art of Presentation: Mastering the art of effective presentations will help you convey ideas confidently and persuasively.

Skillful Qualification: Identifying viable investment prospects is key to making informed decisions and minimizing risks.

Nurturing Relationships: Building strong connections with clients and partners fosters a thriving real estate business.

Database Dynamo: Organizing and managing a comprehensive database will equip you with valuable insights and information.

Niche Navigator: Becoming knowledgeable in niche areas, such as legal matters, adds to your expertise and credibility.

Grit and Determination: Successful investors understand the value of perseverance and dedication when facing setbacks.

Mindset: The Foundation of Real Estate Success

Your mindset is the cornerstone of your rental property investment journey. Before you embark on this path, understand your purpose and what drives you. Whether you seek financial freedom, a secure retirement, or a better life for your loved ones, a clear purpose will fuel your determination.

Imagine yourself in different scenarios – catering to students, providing homes for families, or supporting local businesses. Picture your ideal investment and the impact it will have. This exercise will help you define your goals and align them with your purpose.

To succeed, cultivate qualities like adaptability, decisiveness, and willingness to learn. Embrace a growth mindset that values continuous improvement and acknowledges that success comes with challenges.

Mastering Your Mindset

Your personality plays a significant role in shaping your mindset. Take the time to assess your strengths and weaknesses, both in skills and traits. Seek feedback from trusted sources to gain a comprehensive perspective.

Embrace your uniqueness and focus on how you can leverage your personality to excel in rental property investment. Remember, there is no one-size-fits-all approach to success; it is about refining your path based on your attributes and aspirations.

As you embark on this transformative journey, keep your purpose at the forefront of your mind.

Embrace the power of determination, perseverance, and adaptability. Success in rental property investment lies not only in setting goals but also in fostering a mindset that empowers you to thrive in the face of challenges.

Let your passion be the guiding force as you create a future filled with financial freedom and prosperity.
It is within your reach, and with the right mindset, you will unlock its full potential.

CHAPTER THREE

UNVEILING REAL ESTATE'S WINNING EDGE

As you embark on your investment journey, you'll encounter a plethora of strategies vying for your attention. While the allure of the stock market, bonds, REITs, and cryptocurrencies is undeniable, one investment strategy stands out with its unique advantages—real estate. Let's delve into why real estate prevails over other options and explore the reasons behind its popularity, particularly rental property investments.

Why Real Estate Investment?

Diverse Income Streams: Real estate investments offer multiple avenues for generating income, with rental yield being a prominent source. This yield represents the net income received from rentals after subtracting expenses like taxes and maintenance costs.

Appreciation Potential: Over time, real estate properties tend to appreciate, making them attractive assets. While appreciation rates fluctuate, properties generally appreciate in value, allowing investors to profit when selling.

Inflation Hedge: Real estate can act as a hedge against inflation. As living costs rise, the demand for rental properties tends to increase, enabling landlords to charge higher rents. Meanwhile, fixed mortgage payments lead to enhanced cash flow.

Leverage Opportunities: Real estate enables investors to leverage borrowed funds to acquire larger or additional properties, amplifying their return on investment.

Tax Benefits: Real estate investments offer various tax deductions, including mortgage interest, insurance, maintenance costs, property taxes, and depreciation. These deductions can significantly reduce the overall tax burden.

Types of Real Estate Investment

Fix and Flips: Investors opt for fix and flips by purchasing properties at discounted prices, renovating them, and selling them at a profit.

Rent to Own: This strategy involves renting out a property with an option for the tenant to purchase it at the end of the lease term.

Vacation Rentals: Owning vacation properties and renting them out through platforms like VRBO or Airbnb provides both a getaway spot and rental income.

Commercial Property: Investing in commercial properties and leasing them to businesses offers stable income streams.

Income Properties: Properties acquired primarily for generating rental income fall under this category, encompassing single-family, multi-family, or commercial properties.

Key Calculations for Rental Property Investors

Gross Rent Multiplier (GRM): Investors use the GRM to determine how long it takes for a property to pay for itself based on rental income. A lower GRM indicates a quicker return on investment.

1% Rule: This rule suggests that the monthly gross rent should be at least 1% of the property's purchase price, aiding in assessing its income potential.

Capitalization Rate (Cap Rate): The cap rate reveals the potential return on investment by dividing the net operating income (NOI) by the property's current market value.

Return on Investment (ROI): Calculating the profit relative to the investment cost helps investors assess the performance of their real estate ventures.

Cash-on-Cash Return: This calculation presents the annual return on the actual cash investment, factoring in rental income and expenses.

Real estate's tangibility, stability, and potential for passive income and appreciation set it apart from other investment options like stocks and market-driven assets. While each strategy has its merits, rental property investment's compelling blend of wealth-building advantages, tax incentives, and long-term security make it a preferred choice among investors seeking financial prosperity.

CHAPTER FOUR

THE LANDLORD'S ODYSSEY

Step into the shoes of a modern-day landlord and venture into the uncharted territory of property investment. Prepare to embark on a unique odyssey filled with opportunities for passive income, but also the trials and tribulations of managing rental properties. This chapter will take you on a thrilling journey, experiencing the day-to-day life and monthly adventures of a landlord, while uncovering the secrets to success in this demanding but rewarding realm.

Life on the Horizon

As the sun rises on the horizon, the life of a landlord begins. Each day is an unpredictable voyage, where responsibilities and challenges ebb and flow like the tides. Whether you're a hands-on property manager or you delegate tasks to experts, the key to a smooth sailing lies in efficient communication and collaboration.

Rent collection, the heartbeat of your enterprise, offers both stability and unpredictability. While most tenants adhere to a standard payment schedule, occasional variations can test your adaptability. Prorated rents and flexible payment options may come into play, demanding your strategic finesse.

Utilities pose another set of considerations. Should you include them in the rental fee or let tenants handle them? Your choices not only impact your income stream but also the overall tenant experience, affecting tenant retention and satisfaction.

Navigating the Waters of Monthly Duties

With the new month's arrival comes a fresh set of responsibilities and opportunities. Routine tasks like HVAC filter changes and property maintenance keep your ship afloat, ensuring your investments remain in top-notch condition.

Rent collection becomes a prominent beacon in your monthly voyage. Embracing digital methods and multiple payment options can streamline the process and improve your cash flow, leaving you more time to chart new territories.

Yet, amidst the calm waters, storms may arise. Burst pipes, faulty appliances, or challenging tenants can challenge your resilience. Swiftly addressing these issues and providing timely solutions are vital to maintain the ship's harmony.

Confronting Tempestuous Tenants

The tempestuous seas of problem tenants can cause distress, but equipping yourself with the right strategies will steer you through the turmoil. Building transparent and comprehensive lease agreements from the outset is your anchor, providing a solid foundation to weather potential storms.

Record every interaction and meticulously document tenant communications to safeguard against future disputes. Seeking legal counsel at the early stages can offer invaluable guidance and support, should complications arise.

In the event of late rent payments, approach the matter with a blend of firmness and empathy. Allowing a grace period demonstrates understanding, while enforcing clear consequences for non-payment upholds your rights as a landlord.

Charting a Course for Success

As you traverse the landlord's odyssey, exercise caution and foresight. Extending your reach without proper preparation can lead to treacherous waters. Managing cash flow diligently and making prudent investment decisions are vital to sustaining your journey's momentum.

Be vigilant in your tenant selection process, conducting thorough screenings to avoid potential risks. A well-informed choice can mean the difference between smooth sailing and stormy seas.

Embrace this voyage with a thirst for knowledge and a passion for growth. Each challenge you encounter becomes an opportunity to refine your skills and steer your investments towards prosperity. As you navigate through the landlord's odyssey, you'll find that, with determination and perseverance, the rewards of this unique adventure are truly boundless.

CHAPTER FIVE

THE RHYTHMS OF PROSPERITY IN RENTAL PROPERTY INVESTMENT

In the captivating world of rental property investment, success is a symphony that unfolds with a harmonious interplay of time, effort, and opportunity. As you embark on this melodious journey, let's explore the unique cadence of achievement and the factors that shape the rhythm of prosperity.

The Dance of Progress

In this dynamic landscape, it's natural to desire swift rewards and immediate gains. However, the dance of progress is a nuanced choreography, where each step forward is influenced by a myriad of variables. Your financial goals, resources, and investment strategy all play a significant role in orchestrating the timing of success.

Take a moment to envision your desired outcomes. Do you seek a steady stream of supplementary income, or do you aspire to compose a grand opus of financial independence? Understanding your aspirations and assessing your financial standing will set the tempo for your investment journey.

Tempo and Timing

As with any finely-tuned performance, timing is everything. The tempo at which you progress is intricately woven with market conditions, the availability of suitable properties, and your readiness to seize opportunities. Embrace patience and avoid the allure of hasty decisions, for the crescendo of success builds gradually.

In your symphony of investment, you may encounter tales of individuals who stumbled upon remarkable fortunes overnight, akin to a serendipitous melody. Such anecdotes, however, are rare and often overshadow the dedication and discipline required for sustained success, much like the steady rhythm maintained by seasoned investors.

Each crescendo of achievement is uniquely shaped by your financial position, credit history, and market knowledge. Embrace the learning phase as a virtuoso embraces practice, for it refines your skills and prepares you to compose harmonious investments.

Harmonizing Life's Melodies

Amidst the pursuit of prosperity, life's melodies may introduce unexpected key changes. Work commitments, personal obligations, and family responsibilities can all influence the rhythm of your journey. Finding equilibrium is paramount, as balancing these various melodies is essential for creating a symphony of success.

Consider the time you can dedicate to your investment endeavor each week, but remain flexible, for life's dynamics are ever-changing. In moments when the tempo quickens, your passion for the art of investment will carry you forward, ensuring your pursuit of success remains steadfast.

The Overture of Adaptability

Your symphony of success is an ever-evolving masterpiece. Embrace the art of adaptability as you navigate the harmonies of opportunity and challenges. The tasks you undertake and the time invested may shift, but your unwavering commitment remains the conductor of your journey.

Compose a symphony of success by setting achievable goals, crafting a comprehensive investment strategy, and determining the time you can devote to your passion.

As you embark on this symphonic odyssey, visualize the harmonies of prosperity and let them guide your rhythm towards a crescendo of achievements.

Remember, success is subjective, much like the beauty found in diverse musical compositions.
Define what success means to you, and let it resonate through your every decision and endeavor.
The rhythm of rental property investment dances to the beat of your passion, knowledge, and dedication.
Embrace the melody of this journey, and the grand symphony of success shall be yours to orchestrate.

CHAPTER SIX

THE ART OF RENTAL PROPERTY SYMPHONY

Imagine yourself as the conductor of an orchestra, poised to lead a captivating symphony that echoes the path to rental property investing success. This chapter unveils a fresh perspective on how to embark on this exhilarating journey, where your financial prowess, mindset, and creativity converge to compose a unique melody of prosperity.

Opening Notes: A Harmonious Start

As you take your first steps into the realm of rental property investing, the key is commitment and the drive to build wealth through real estate. For most beginners, investing in properties with one to four units offers a safe and steady start. But the question remains: How do you transition from a potential investor to a seasoned conductor orchestrating a successful real estate symphony?

The Mentorship Sonata: A Guiding Hand

In the realm of investment virtuosos, mentors play an indispensable role—seasoned artists willing to share their experience and expertise. Seek out a real estate mentor who can guide you through your first deal and help you decipher the complex notes of the industry.

Mentoring relationships have echoed through generations, nurturing growth and nurturing the flame of knowledge. But remember, not all mentors are equal, and finding the right one is key. Look for someone who shares your passion and investment goals, forming a melodious bond that harmonizes your success.

Conducting the Melody: Your Symphony of Deals

With your mentor by your side, you venture into the vast repertoire of investment opportunities. While traditional methods often involve realtors and bank loans, your unique approach involves finding properties independently.

Rather than waiting for a realtor's cue, explore alternative channels to discover hidden gems. Craigslist, online platforms, and local meetings offer a treasure trove of offbeat properties waiting for their moment in the spotlight. Embrace the thrill of the hunt, and let each property be a crescendo in your investment journey.

Transcending Limits: The Real Estate Overture

For those seeking to amplify their investment repertoire, obtaining a real estate license can elevate your performance. With a license, you gain access to the Multiple Listing Service (MLS) database and the opportunity to sell properties without paying commissions to others.

However, remember that with great power comes great responsibility. As a licensed agent, your ethical harmony must remain impeccable, embracing transparency and full disclosure in every deal.

The Crescendo of Your Symphony

As you embrace your role as conductor and virtuoso, remember that every symphony is a unique expression of its creator. Your journey as a rental property investor is your personal concerto, and each note played contributes to your opus of prosperity.

Harmonize your commitment, knowledge, and passion, and let the crescendo of success resound through the halls of real estate. With each investment, you perfect your composition, and the melody of prosperity weaves through your life.

So, take up the baton and lead your symphony of rental property success. Embrace the magic of mentorship, dance to the rhythm of your research, and let your investment portfolio become a masterpiece of wealth and achievement.

As the curtains rise on your symphonic journey, the stage is set for you to create your opus of prosperity—a timeless composition of rental property investing mastery. Let the music of your success echo through the annals of real estate history, inspiring future virtuosos to follow in your harmonious footsteps.

CHAPTER SEVEN

UNRAVELING THE SECRETS OF PROPERTY CLASSES

Embarking on the journey of real estate investment is akin to navigating a labyrinth of property classes, each holding its own allure and challenges. As a budding investor, understanding the intricate dynamics of these classes is the key to unlocking a world of opportunities and building a thriving portfolio.

Class A: The Crown Jewel

Picture yourself stepping into a realm of opulence, where modernity and sophistication blend seamlessly—a Class A property.

These magnificent abodes, recently built or thoughtfully restored historical gems, boast state-of-the-art amenities and exquisite finishes. While they exude prestige, they come with a steep price tag and offer relatively lower cash flow. For aspiring investors, Class A properties may seem like a distant dream, but their allure remains undeniable.

Class B: The Balance of Potential

In the symphony of real estate, Class B properties strike the perfect balance between value and potential. These slightly older, well-maintained homes exude a sense of charm and hold the promise of a fruitful investment. With a better capitalization rate than Class A, they offer a chance for steady cash flow and growth. As the conductor of your investment journey, consider Class B as the sweet spot, where harmony meets opportunity.

Class C: The Melody of Discovery

Venturing into Class C properties is like uncovering hidden treasures in the real estate realm. These aged homes, often over 30 years old, may require some tender loving care, but they present unique opportunities for the astute investor.

Nestled in less glamorous neighborhoods with a lower-income tenant base, Class C properties may require more management and repairs. Yet, their potential for high cash flow and rewarding investments make them an intriguing composition for those willing to explore.

Class D: The Crescendo of Challenge

Prepare to embrace the crescendo of risk as you delve into Class D properties. These aged buildings, usually in a state of disrepair, demand extensive renovations and careful handling. Class D investments are not for the faint of heart, as they come with higher risks and significant challenges. Investors with a seasoned ear for real estate may find hidden gems in these properties, but beginners should approach with caution and seek guidance from experienced mentors.

Fine-Tuning Your Investment Symphony

As you compose your investment symphony, consider the specific tempo that suits your aspirations and circumstances. For novice investors, Class B properties often present a harmonious starting point, offering a blend of affordability and potential for growth.

To identify the perfect property class, explore various online platforms and attend local meetings to learn about available opportunities. Listen to the market's melody, and make wise decisions based on thorough research and analysis. As your expertise grows, you may venture into other property classes, fine-tuning your investment composition.

Conducting Your Legacy

In this grand symphony of real estate investing, you take the baton, guiding the melody of your success. Embrace the diversity of property classes, each presenting a unique tune to compose your opus of prosperity.

As you progress through the movements of real estate investing, remember to stay agile and adaptable. Learn from every note played, adjusting your composition as market dynamics change. Seek the guidance of experienced mentors, the virtuosos of the real estate world, who can help you navigate the intricacies of each class.

With every investment, you add a new note to your symphony of wealth-building, leaving a lasting legacy of financial achievement.

CHAPTER EIGHT

THE DIVERSE CANVAS OF RENTAL PROPERTY VENTURES

Venturing into the realm of rental property investing is akin to stepping into a vast canvas adorned with a myriad of investment types. Each stroke of opportunity brings forth a fresh perspective and a wealth of possibilities. Let us embark on a journey to explore the fascinating tapestry of residential, commercial, and retail properties, each holding a unique key to prosperity.

Residential, Commercial, and Retail: A Trifecta of Opportunities

The exploration begins with the triad of property types: residential, commercial, and retail. Residential properties offer a sanctuary to single families, while commercial spaces embrace businesses that seek a place to flourish. Retail properties, on the other hand, beckon with the allure of bustling commercial ventures. Within this trinity lies a plethora of investment potential, awaiting your discerning eye.

Discovering the Charm of Condos and Townhomes

As we venture into the residential domain, the enchanting world of condos and townhomes unfurls. Condos, nestled within larger structures or office complexes, offer a unique blend of privacy and shared amenities, creating an appealing prospect for prospective tenants. Meanwhile, townhomes exude individuality with shared walls, fostering a sense of community among residents.

In this realm of allure, condos and townhomes beckon as ideal entry points for budding investors. With a smaller investment and a pool of potential renters, these properties hold the promise of steady returns. Yet, tread cautiously, as high HOA fees and stringent regulations may influence your decision.

Single-Family Homes: The Epitome of Stability

As we turn our gaze to the single-family home segment, a symphony of stability unfolds. From charming ranch-style dwellings to multi-level masterpieces, the diverse array of single-family homes caters to various tenant preferences. Seeking properties in up-and-coming neighborhoods or near bustling college campuses ensures a steady stream of potential renters.

In this harmonious composition, investing in Class B properties in emerging areas holds the key to scaling your investment portfolio over time. Embrace the dynamic rhythm of market trends, aligning your investment with the ever-evolving demands of your tenants.

Multi-Family Real Estate: A Chorus of Versatility

The grand stage of multi-family units takes center stage, encompassing townhouse buildings, duplexes, apartments, and homes with separate rental units. This versatile ensemble offers a range of investment possibilities, catering to both seasoned investors and newcomers seeking supplementary income.

Within this multifaceted chorus, consider the art of "house-hacking," where residing in part of the multi-family property supports your investment journey while renting out the remaining units. This innovative approach not only bolsters your investment but also strengthens your mortgage application.

REOs and Foreclosures: Unveiling Hidden Treasures

In the crescendo of our exploration, the world of REOs and foreclosures emerges as a captivating overture of opportunity.

REOs, properties foreclosed by banks, offer the chance to uncover hidden treasures awaiting revitalization. While these properties may require extensive refurbishment, they boast potential for both rentals and fix-and-flip ventures.

Enter this realm with caution, as deals vary based on location, occasion, and individual requirements. Patience and perseverance shall lead you to REO treasures worthy of your investment.

Fixer-Uppers: Orchestrating the Melody of Transformation

As our symphony reaches its climax, fixer-uppers play a pivotal role, crafting a melody of transformation. These unassuming properties offer the canvas for creating rental havens with a touch of restoration. However, balance is essential, as over-investment can lead to diminished returns.

Navigate the world of fixer-uppers with finesse, considering both fix-and-flip opportunities and long-term rentals. Embrace the challenge of renovation while keeping the harmony of profitability at the core of your investment.

Harmony Amidst Diversity: Your Investment Symphony

As the conductor of your investment symphony, harmonize the diverse property types with your aspirations and financial capacity. Embrace the beauty of diversity, for in the symphony of property types lies the melody of prosperity, waiting to be orchestrated by your unwavering passion for real estate.

In this enthralling world of rental property investing, let your creativity and determination lead you to a crescendo of financial success. Embrace the ever-evolving canvas of opportunities, discovering hidden gems, and learning from the symphony of experienced mentors.

As your investment symphony unfurls, may it resound with the notes of prosperity, painting a canvas of success and fulfillment in the realm of rental property ventures.

CHAPTER NINE

UNVEILING THE ENIGMA OF LOCATION IN REAL ESTATE INVESTMENT

In the enigmatic world of real estate investment, the age-old mantra "location, location, location" reverberates with a profound sense of importance. Whether you are an experienced investor or a curious newcomer, the choice of location holds the key to unlocking the full potential of your investment journey. Let us embark on a quest to unravel the secrets of location, exploring the possibilities of local and remote investments, and discovering the hidden gems that lie within.

Local vs. Remote Investments: The Dichotomy of Pros and Cons

Within the vast realm of real estate, two distinct paths beckon to aspiring investors: local investments that nestle close to home and remote ventures that take them far beyond their comfort zones. Each path carries its own allure, accompanied by a plethora of advantages and disadvantages that demand careful contemplation.

Local investments provide a competitive edge, leveraging the investor's deep knowledge of the community and the local market. Intimate familiarity with the area can prove to be a valuable asset, helping investors make well-informed decisions and outshine absentee landlords. Proximity to the rental property empowers investors to address any issues promptly, ensuring a smoother investment experience.

On the other hand, the allure of remote investments lies in the excitement of exploring uncharted territories and tapping into new markets. However, navigating the challenges of investing from a distance requires a strategic approach and meticulous planning to mitigate potential disadvantages.

Unraveling the Significance of Location: The Nexus of Value and Purpose

At the heart of location lies the intricate interplay between value and purpose. As you venture forth on your investment odyssey, value manifests in two distinctive forms: the appreciation of your primary residence and the potential income generated by rental properties. Understanding these distinct forms of value becomes the compass guiding your investment choices.

The canvas of real estate investment comes alive with the artistry of fixer-uppers, where minimizing initial investment while maximizing property value becomes the ultimate goal. Flippers and speculators seek hidden gems, undervalued properties brimming with untapped potential.

Price to Rent Ratio: Decoding the Melody of Investment

In the symphony of real estate investment, calculations and ratios dance in harmony. The Price to Rent Ratio emerges as a powerful metric, shedding light on the relationship between property price and rental potential. A low ratio signals a promising investment with significant rental potential, while a high ratio prompts cautious consideration.

Embarking on a Data Expedition

The pursuit of knowledge in the realm of location research takes investors on an exhilarating data expedition. Unraveling the mysteries of population size, demographics, unemployment rates, household income, housing prices, and interest rates becomes an essential quest. Trusted sources like neighborhooddiscount.com, realtor.com, and nar.realtor serve as guides through this labyrinth of data.

In Conclusion: The Symphony of Location

As our journey into the enigmatic world of location draws to a close, may you embrace the profound significance of this artistry within real estate investing. The symphony of location orchestrates the cadence of value, the melody of investment, and the harmonies of opportunity. Embrace the power of location as the guiding conductor of your investment symphony, leading you towards a symphony of prosperity and success in the world of real estate.

CHAPTER TEN

THE QUEST FOR RENTAL PROPERTY BRILLIANCE

Beyond the conventional classifications of real estate, lies a realm of untapped potential—the elusive brilliance of rental properties. As you journey into this captivating world, let's explore the key factors that can unlock unprecedented success and captivate both tenants and investors alike.

Rooms: The Soul of Tenant Satisfaction

In the enchanting realm of rental properties, the number of rooms holds the key to tenant contentment. While one and two-bedroom houses may have their allure, they often lead to frequent tenant turnover. To ensure lasting tenancy and stable rental income, consider properties with at least three bedrooms, perfect for accommodating families seeking a long-term home.

The Ageless Dilemma: Historic Charm vs. Modern Efficiency

The allure of a historic home steeped in charm can be magnetic, but seasoned investors are well aware of the challenges that accompany such properties. While older homes may boast architectural splendor, they may also entail higher repair costs and inefficiency in utility usage. Striking the perfect balance between charm and modern efficiency is paramount. Opt for properties with modern amenities and energy-saving features to appeal to a broader tenant base and ensure cost-effective operations.

The Garage Enigma

In the mystical world of single-family rentals, the garage holds an enigmatic allure that bewitches tenants.

Whether it's a safe haven for their car or a storage sanctuary, tenants highly value the convenience of a garage. Properties with this coveted amenity can foster longer tenant stays and heighten overall tenant satisfaction.

Utilities: A Delicate Dance

The delicate dance of utilities revolves around one crucial question: who bears the burden of payment? While some tenants appreciate the convenience of utilities included in the rent, it often leads to careless usage and higher expenses for landlords. Encourage tenant responsibility by having them cover utilities, while keeping rents competitive. Alternatively, explore master-metered systems to monitor and fairly allocate utility costs.

The Garden of Serenity

A tranquil outdoor space can transform a rental property into a serene retreat. Tenants cherish the opportunity to host gatherings, relish barbecues, and bask in the beauty of a well-maintained garden. Investing in properties with captivating outdoor spaces can attract and retain tenants, especially those seeking a haven to call home.

Parking: A Coveted Convenience

The availability of parking can be the tipping point for potential tenants. Ensure your rental properties offer sufficient parking spaces, ideally providing two spots per unit. Ample parking not only enhances tenant satisfaction but also increases the allure of your property to a broader audience.

Proximity to Amenities: The Magic of Convenience

In this mystical realm, the allure of nearby amenities holds a bewitching power over renters. A neighborhood's safety, proximity to parks, schools, grocery stores, and easy commutes to work can elevate your rental property's appeal and ignite tenant demand.

The Quest for the Perfect Investment

As you embark on your quest for brilliance, explore diverse avenues that can lead to triumph. Existing multi-family dwellings, such as apartments or mobile home parks, offer intriguing opportunities for small investors. Seek out potential deals in foreclosures, where affordable properties beckon with the promise of improvement. Steer clear of the daunting world of land and building construction, with its substantial initial investment and prolonged timelines.

In Conclusion: Embrace the Brilliance

As you tread further into this captivating landscape of rental properties, embrace the brilliance that lies within each decision. Let the allure of tenant satisfaction, efficient properties, and enchanting amenities guide your choices. With each step, you will unlock the secrets to a thriving and mesmerizing rental property portfolio. Let this quest be your path to unparalleled success in the wondrous realm of real estate investment.

CHAPTER ELEVEN

THE ENCHANTING ART OF PROPERTY PROWESS

In the realm of real estate, a sorcerer's wisdom lies in the art of deal analysis. As you navigate the mystic world of potential properties, a trove of unique tools and captivating insights awaits, ready to unveil the true essence of each investment.

Embracing the Digital Grimoire

Harness the power of the digital grimoire, where online tools like "Prophecy Analyzer" reveal the hidden secrets of rental properties. Unravel the property's history, location, and investment potential with a mere tap. From cash flow conjurations to IRR incantations, the grimoire holds the key to unlocking the property's true value.

The Triad of Illumination: Income, Expenses, and Fair Market Magic

Within the sacred triad of income, expenses, and fair market magic, lies the essence of a profitable venture. Peer into the crystal ball of adjusted income, where gross scheduled income reveals its true potential minus 10%. Next, conjure the expenses, ensuring a harmonious balance between gains and costs. Finally, let the incantation of fair market value reveal the property's true worth.

The Quest for Hidden Gems

As you embark on your quest, seek hidden gems and rare opportunities. Channel your inner alchemist to transmute properties with untapped potential into golden investments. But beware, for the allure of overpayment can ensnare even the most seasoned sorcerer. Only those who resist such temptation shall thrive.

The Enigma of Cash Flow and Appreciation

In the labyrinth of real estate, the eternal enigma of cash flow versus appreciation beckons. Each path holds its allure, but the wise sorcerer knows their true calling. Let your intuition guide you, whether to cherish the immediate rewards of cash flow or the promise of future appreciation. Your chosen path shall reveal the essence of your investment style.

Unraveling the Alchemical Expenses

Behold the alchemical expenses that vary from land to land, shrouded in mystery and intrigue. Unveil the key costs: PITI, utilities, maintenance, and more. Each holds a secret that can make or break a venture. With careful calculation, the sorcerer can decipher the true essence of property expenses.

The Enchantment of Analysis

With knowledge as your staff and intuition as your compass, cast the enchantment of analysis on the lands you seek to conquer. Unravel the mystical numbers, and let the metrics weave their spell. The journey of property analysis is a captivating tale, where data and intuition dance in harmony, revealing the path to prosperity in the world of real estate sorcery.

CHAPTER TWELVE

UNRAVELING THE REAL ESTATE ODYSSEY

Embarking on a journey to find the perfect investment deals is like setting sail on an epic odyssey, where adventure and opportunity await at every turn. As you navigate the vast seas of the property market, armed with practical wisdom and keen insights, you shall uncover hidden treasures and forge your path to success.

Charting New Territories

Like an intrepid explorer, your first step is to choose a geographic target market and define the type of property you seek. With your course set, the quest to identify potential acquisitions begins. But fear not, for the realm of real estate offers a myriad of avenues to explore.

The Enigmatic MLS and Ancient Newspapers

The enigmatic MLS, a treasure trove of properties listed by brokers far and wide, beckons you with its alluring possibilities. But do not overlook the wisdom of the ancients, for within the fading pages of newspapers lie whispers of off-market deals, waiting to be discovered.

Whispers on the Wind

In this age of digital wonders, the ancient art of word of mouth remains a potent ally. Letting people know you are in search of rentals opens doorways to unexpected connections. A neighbor's hushed revelation of their intent to sell might lead to a mutually beneficial arrangement.

Mystical Encounters on Craigslist

Venturing into the virtual realm of Craigslist can be an encounter with the mystical and the mundane. As you sift through its offerings, you may uncover genuine deals amidst the murk of potential scams. But with diligence and discernment, you shall find the true gems.

Conjuring the Sellers

Masters of the trade know the power of outbound marketing, summoning sellers to their call. Armed with advertisements and direct mail, you weave spells of attraction that draw prospective sellers to your cause. A real estate license acts as your enchanted staff, heightening your allure to the sellers.

The Enchanted Loopnet

In the realm of commercial properties and multi-family dwellings, the enchanted Loopnet weaves its magic. Here, shopping malls and fast-food establishments reveal their hidden potential. Delve into this realm with care, for great rewards await the discerning seeker.

The Art of Divination: Property Screening

As you gather your potential treasures, the art of property screening becomes your divination tool. Casting your criteria like runes, you discern the perfect location, property type, condition, and class. Through this mystical process, you narrow your choices to the most promising prospects.

The Visionary Portal: Virtual Surveys

The universe bestows upon you the visionary portal of virtual surveys, granting glimpses into the future. 3D tours and captivating images unravel the essence of the properties, guiding your choices. But should the veil remain elusive, the sacred on-site survey unveils the truths hidden within.

Embrace the Odyssey

As you traverse the realm of real estate on your odyssey to find your first and subsequent deals, embrace the adventure with an open heart and a daring spirit. The universe shall reward your boldness with hidden gems and boundless opportunities. Let the magic of the market guide you, and may your journey be a triumphant saga of success.

CHAPTER THIRTEEN

THE KEYS TO UNLOCKING REAL ESTATE SUCCESS

In the realm of real estate, a myriad of paths awaits those seeking their first deal. As you embark on this thrilling journey, it's essential to explore the various purchase methods, each offering a unique blend of advantages and challenges.

Diverse Investment Strategies

The real estate world brims with an array of investment strategies, each holding its allure and potential. From raising capital through partnerships to the lease-to-own approach, the possibilities are vast. Understanding the risks and returns will empower you to make informed decisions and steer your path to success.

Raising Capital through Partnerships

Forming partnerships opens doors to higher cash flow and exponential growth potential. Collaborating with knowledgeable and experienced individuals can optimize your real estate ventures. However, sharing control and profits demands trust and a strong partnership. Choosing reliable partners can lead to rewarding outcomes.

Embracing the Lease-to-Own Approach

The lease-to-own approach unveils a unique opportunity to acquire properties from homeowners facing mortgage difficulties. By offering a lease-to-own deal, you help tenants who aspire to be homeowners but are hindered by cash or credit constraints. This two-stage process can lead to quick returns or long-term investments, depending on market conditions.

Unveiling the Power of Owner Financing

Owner financing offers an intriguing option to reduce down payments and expedite property transactions. Sellers assume the role of the bank, enabling you to bridge the financial gap required for purchase. This captivating arrangement can be a lifeline for buyers unable to secure traditional mortgages.

Unlocking Mortgage Assumptions

In the realm of mortgage assumptions, you take on the responsibility of the existing mortgage payments. The original mortgage holder is released from liability, and you become the payer.

This option becomes more appealing when it offers better mortgage rates than those available from traditional lenders.

Harmonizing Deferred Maintenance Credits

Deferred maintenance credits add a touch of enchantment to real estate deals. By accepting credits for necessary repairs during closing, you open doors to property improvements and increased investment potential.

The Enchanting World of Escrow and Reserve Accounts

Escrow accounts hold the promise of a smooth transaction, ensuring funds are securely deposited until closing. Reserve accounts act as safeguards to guarantee adherence to sale conditions and meet mortgage company requirements.

Prorated Rent: A Symphony of Cash Flow

Prorated rent emerges as a melodious source of cash flow. By calculating rents to cover all days of the month, investors can maximize their income and facilitate property acquisitions.

Unleashing the Power of Security Deposits

Security deposits hold the keys to cash flow and investment potential. While they can provide a financial cushion, investors must exercise caution in their usage to avoid potential complications.

Sharing Closing Costs in Harmony

In the spirit of cooperation, buyers and sellers can share closing costs, lightening the financial burden for both parties and fostering a smooth transition to property ownership.

The Magic of Real Estate Syndication

Real estate syndication gathers a multitude of investors, pooling funds to explore new opportunities and ventures. With the potential for acquisition fees, asset management fees, and equity participation, syndication can lead to mutual prosperity and financial success.

Harnessing the Strength of LLCs

Limited Liability Companies (LLCs) offer robust protection and tax benefits for real estate investors.

Shielding from financial storms, LLCs elevate real estate endeavors to new heights, ensuring a secure path to success.

The Symphony of Loan Types

From the timeless thirty-year fixed mortgage to FHA loans and primary lenders, the symphony of loan types presents a range of choices for investors. Each option holds its unique charm, offering various benefits for financial prosperity.

Unraveling the Tapestry of PMI

The intricate tapestry of Private Mortgage Insurance (PMI) can influence investment decisions. Understanding PMI intricacies helps investors navigate the path to financial success and unlocks new possibilities.

As you embark on your real estate journey, let your heart guide you. Each purchase method holds its allure and potential, offering a magical adventure towards unlocking the keys to real estate success. Embrace the enchantment of diverse strategies, and forge your path to prosperity in the realm of real estate.

CHAPTER FOURTEEN

UNCONVENTIONAL ROUTES TO REALIZE YOUR HOMEOWNERSHIP DREAM

For aspiring homeowners, achieving that elusive down payment can often feel like an insurmountable challenge. But fear not, for there exists an array of creative and resourceful ways to turn your dream of homeownership into reality. Buckle up as we explore 15 unique approaches to securing that cherished down payment:

401k Withdrawal Leap: Though costly, withdrawing funds from your 401k can be balanced with astute investments and timely reimbursements.

HELOC Journey: If you already own a home, consider tapping into its equity through a Home Equity Line of Credit (HELOC) to fund your next property investment.

RELOC Adventure: Utilize the equity from an existing rental property with a Rental Equity Line of Credit (RELOC) to bolster your down payment.

Cross-Collateralization Expedition: Explore putting a lien against a property to apply for a new loan, using the lien as the down payment.

Roth IRA Expedition: Navigate the world of Roth IRAs, withdrawing from one for your first home purchase while ensuring you meet the criteria to avoid fees.

House Hacking Trailblaze: Opt for a duplex or multi-family home, rent out a portion, and use the rental income to cover the mortgage.

Seller Financing Odyssey: Embark on a journey of seller or owner financing, simplifying the process of obtaining a traditional loan.

Personal Loans Quest: Reach out to friends and family for personal loans to bolster your down payment fund.

Co-Investing Exploration: Team up with family or friends willing to contribute to your down payment goal.

Sell Your Belongings Quest: While not a full solution, selling belongings can significantly contribute to your down payment fund.

Credit Card Adventure: Venture into the realm of credit cards for quick funds, but be cautious of fees and their impact on your credit score.

Debt Clearance Trek: Forge ahead by prioritizing the payoff of high-interest debts to unlock monthly income for savings.

Quantitative Methods Voyage: Offer your expertise to other investors, gaining acquisition fees by presenting profitable properties.

Fix and Flip Endeavor: Embark on a fix-and-flip journey to raise capital for your dream home.

Refinancing Voyage: Set sail on the seas of refinancing after renovating your current home to unlock increased equity.

Mapping Your First House Budget

The amount needed for your first house depends on various factors, including deal structure, down payment, and selling price.

While some options require zero down payment, others involve external funding sources. Additionally, remember to consider additional fees like realtor and lawyer charges, typically amounting to 3 - 4% of the home's purchase price.

Buyers should also take into account title search, insurance, record, and legal fees. By strategizing and negotiating, you may uncover deals where sellers willingly cover these costs, enabling you to minimize your overall investment.

Borrowing with Qualifying Collateral

In some cases, you can explore borrowing the down payment using collateral accepted by another financial institution. This strategic move allows you to leverage existing assets to secure the funds required for your homeownership dreams.

Ultimately, the journey to homeownership is a thrilling adventure filled with creativity and financial acumen. By embracing these diverse methods, you can pave your way to your dream home and embark on a path to a prosperous future. Remember, with a dash of innovation and determination, every obstacle can become an opportunity on your route to homeownership bliss.

CHAPTER FIFTEEN

MASTERING THE FINANCIAL NEXUS - A ROADMAP TO MORTGAGE TRIUMPH

Embarking on your real estate investment journey, you soon realize the importance of forming solid alliances with banks. In today's post-credit crisis landscape, securing mortgage funds demands finesse and adherence to stringent criteria. Collaborating with the right lender can become your most valuable asset in this competitive landscape.

Cracking the Code: Deciphering Bank Prerequisites

Financial qualifications set by banks serve as the gateway to funding your dreams. Essential criteria typically encompass:

A down payment ranging from twenty to twenty-five percent of the property's value.

A credit score of 740 or higher, showcasing your creditworthiness.

Maintaining a debt-to-income ratio of 36% or lower, demonstrating your financial stability.

While mortgage brokers and bankers may seem like viable options, exercise caution to avoid hefty fees that might undermine your investment potential. Whenever possible, direct engagement with banks is the preferred route.

The Qualification Quest: Mapping Your Loan Application

Your journey towards securing a loan involves a comprehensive application process, necessitating the provision of essential information such as:

Bank application form
Executive summary
Current rent details
Historical financials (2 to 3 years of income, and at least one year of bank statements)
Copy of leases attached to the property
Copy of purchase agreement
Pro forma financials
Real estate schedule
Business financials

State and federal tax returns

For emerging investors, where business documentation might be limited, focus on furnishing personal details, a copy of the LLC and any financial contributions made to the company.

Work closely with your loan officer to fine-tune the application to meet your specific deal requirements.

Navigating the Underwriting Terrain

Once your application is in, the underwriters meticulously assess it, factoring in your business plan, down payment, and real estate schedule to determine the loan amount. Prepare for potential lender contingencies that include:

Appraisal to validate the property's value.

Environmental reports to ensure the property is free from harmful elements.

Property condition assessment by a third-party contractor.

Title insurance to protect both you and the lender from legal claims.

Tenant estoppel certificates, relevant if tenants already occupy or plan to move in post-sale.

Insurance binder as evidence of minimum coverage amounts.

Property survey to ascertain property lines.

Borrow documents, including resolutions and certificates of good standing.

By understanding these contingencies, you can navigate the loan process effectively and steer it towards a successful closing.

The Art of Building Relationships

Fostering a robust relationship with your bank is an art form. Endeavor to build trust and credibility, as it can pave the way for seamless transactions and more favorable opportunities. If your loan application faces setbacks, address any high-risk factors like credit scores, financial history, or property concerns to refine your approach.

With strategic prowess and skillful navigation, collaborating with banks becomes a rewarding experience, unearthing the funds essential to propel your real estate endeavors to triumph. Remember, a solid partnership with a bank lays the foundation for a flourishing real estate portfolio.

CHAPTER SIXTEEN

MASTERING THE REAL ESTATE DANCE - FROM VISION TO REALITY

With a property in sight and determination in your heart, you're ready to take the plunge into your first real estate investment. The road ahead may seem daunting, but armed with the right knowledge and mindset, you'll navigate this thrilling journey to success.

Step 1: Crafting a Captivating Offer

Your offer is the gateway to your dream property. Three approaches to consider are:

The Enchanting Proposal: Present a non-binding term sheet that outlines your vision and transaction structure, captivating the seller's interest.

The Confident Letter: Opt for a legally binding Letter of Intent for more complex deals. This solidifies your intent while providing leeway for inspections and contingencies.

The Committed Agreement: When confident in your decision, a Purchase Agreement seals the deal with escrow money and a definitive closing timeline.

Begin with a Letter of Intent to secure your position while leaving room for negotiation. Strike a balance between protecting your interests and appealing to the seller's sensibilities.

Step 2: Diligence: Unearthing Hidden Gems

Before sealing the deal, meticulous due diligence is essential. Analyze potential returns, calculate Net Operating Income (NOI), evaluate Gross Rent Multiplier (GRM), and project cash flows. Consider paying a reasonable due diligence fee to safeguard your investment.

Employ seasoned inspectors or contractors, solicit insurance quotes, and gather crucial property data for a well-informed decision.

Step 3: Choosing a Stellar Property Manager

Managing a property from afar requires an exceptional property manager. When making your selection, evaluate their experience, fee structure, tenant screening process, and vacancy rates of other properties they manage. A diligent property manager is the guardian of your investment.

Step 4: Securing the Perfect Financing

As you approach lenders, equip yourself with the right questions to secure favorable financing. Inquire about terms, Loan-to-Value (LTV) ratios, interest rates, fixed-term options, costs, and whether personal guarantees are necessary. A well-prepared approach enhances your approval chances.

Step 5: Embrace the Closing Act

With financing secured, the closing process commences. Carefully review the purchase agreement, set a signing date, arrange funds transfer, and gather necessary documents. Scrutinize every detail, supply required identification and insurance, and be prepared for a life-changing moment.

Remember, every investment journey is unique. Embrace flexibility, stay attuned to opportunities, and let your passion for real estate lead the way. The stage is set, the spotlight awaits; it's time to dazzle the world of real estate with your brilliance!

CHAPTER SEVENTEEN

UNLEASHING THE RENOVATION MAGIC

Welcome to the world of transformation, where your investment property is about to undergo a magical makeover. Get ready to embark on a journey of creativity and innovation as you turn your property into a masterpiece that captivates both tenants and the market.

1. The Visionary Touch: Customizing for Success

Before you put on your renovation hat, envision your dream tenant. Tailor your upgrades to suit their preferences and needs. By focusing on improvements that add significant value and appeal, you'll ensure a well-crafted investment.

2. Enchanting Curb Appeal

The first impression is everything. Spruce up the exterior with a fresh coat of paint, vibrant landscaping, and elegant lighting. A captivating curb appeal will attract tenants like moths to a flame.

3. The Kitchen and Bath Elegance

Kitchens and bathrooms hold the key to a tenant's heart. Invest in modern fixtures, stylish cabinetry, and luxurious countertops. Create a haven of relaxation with spa-like bathrooms and a culinary paradise in the kitchen.

4. Low-Maintenance Wonders

A well-maintained property is a dream for both tenants and landlords. Address any repairs or maintenance concerns proactively to avoid surprises later on. A hassle-free property ensures long-lasting tenancy.

5. The Efficiency Enchantment

Efficiency upgrades are both eco-friendly and budget-friendly. Consider energy-efficient windows, smart thermostats, and water-saving fixtures. Tenants will appreciate the lower utility bills, and you'll enjoy reduced operating costs.

6. Craftsmanship Conjuring

Quality craftsmanship is the secret ingredient that elevates your property. Partner with skilled professionals who take pride in their work. From small details to major renovations, every touch of excellence adds value.

7. The Personal Spell

Infuse your property with a touch of magic - your personality. Select interior designs and color palettes that resonate with your target audience. Create an ambiance that feels like home and sparks an emotional connection.

8. The Transformation Revelation

As your renovation vision takes shape, witness the enchanting transformation of your property. Watch it come to life, exuding charm and allure. The market will be spellbound by your creation.

9. Adapting to the Ever-Changing Realm

Real estate is a dynamic world, ever-evolving with market trends and tenant demands. Stay ahead of the curve by being open to change and embracing new ideas. Flexibility is the key to enduring success.

10. The Enchanted Future

Step into the enchanted future of your investment property. A world of possibilities awaits as you welcome tenants into their dream home. Embrace the magic of renovation, where dreams become reality, and your investment shines brightly in the real estate realm.

Let's delve into the art of networking and discover how it can transform your investment venture:

1. The Magic of a Phone Call

Initiating a phone call to a realtor is an excellent starting point. Craft a compelling introduction, expressing your interest in a long-term partnership for real estate investments. Share your target price range and property preferences, such as multi-unit homes or apartments. Request an appointment to discuss your investment goals and outline your business strategy.

2. Building Bridges: Establishing Your Network

The key to making progress is creating a robust network. Engage with various real estate agencies in your target investment area until you find the perfect match. Building these connections will open doors to valuable opportunities and insights.

3. Mastering the Down Payment Dilemma

Now, let's address the all-important down payment. Assess your financial situation to determine if you have the required funds or if you need investors to join your venture. Craft an opening pitch for landlord associations, highlighting your enthusiasm to learn the ropes from experienced mentors.

4. The Art of the Cold-Email

Apart from phone calls, crafting well-structured cold-emails can help you garner attention. Begin with genuine flattery, mentioning relevant information about the recipient, such as a blog, book, or success story. Concisely state your investment goals and how their guidance could be invaluable. End the email with a call to action, inviting them to connect and provide resources.

5. Embrace the Journey

As you embark on this exciting journey, remember that it is a process of growth and learning. Take time each day to explore potential properties while continuously expanding your network. Enjoy the progress you make as you work towards your ultimate goal.

6. The Afterword: A Foundation for Success

A solid foundation is the bedrock of rental property investments. Your mindset is paramount in driving you towards your first property purchase and long-term success. Equipped with the right knowledge, stable goals, and a strong network, you are poised for success.

7. Embracing Challenges

Owning rental properties comes with its share of challenges, from repairs to problem tenants. However, by leveraging market analysis and passive income strategies, you can ensure consistent monthly income and potentially early retirement.

8. The Tools of the Trade

Throughout this journey, you have acquired essential tools to excel in rental property investment. You possess a deep understanding of property classes and types, enabling you to make informed decisions based on your starting capital. Armed with formulas for analyzing deals and assessing their fair market value, you are prepared for success.

9. Building Your Dream Team

Remember the importance of working with the right team. From real estate professionals to banks and investors, your network will play a vital role in executing successful deals. Approach them with confidence and purpose, ensuring that your collaborations lead to fruitful outcomes.

10. Embrace the Mindset

As you conclude this chapter, remember the invaluable lesson: success begins with your mindset. Firmly believe in the potential of your rental property investment business even before acquiring your first property. Embrace the magic within, and watch your dreams turn into reality.

Epilogue: A Journey of Enchantment

As you leave the realms of this book and venture into the world of real estate investment, keep in mind that this journey is yours to shape and create. Embrace every twist and turn, learn from challenges, and savor the moments of triumph. With dedication, determination, and the power of meaningful connections, you hold the keys to make your mark!

www.ingramcontent.com/pod-product-compliance
Lightning Source LLC
Chambersburg PA
CBHW062253290526
45794CB00006B/2538